W9-AZW-281

What Is **FAITH**?

by Virginia Mueller

illustrated by Kathryn Hutton

Sixth Printing, 1990

©1980, The STANDARD PUBLISHING Company, Cincinnati, Ohio
Division of STANDEX INTERNATIONAL Corporation. Printed in U.S.A.

Faith is seeing
with your heart
what you cannot see
with your eyes.

It is planting a seed
and hoping for a flower.

It is finding a caterpillar

and believing that someday it will fly.

It is counting the eggs in a nest
and trusting they will hatch.

Sometimes faith is planning
for tomorrow today.

Faith is counting
the days
until your birthday.

Faith is looking forward to being big.

Faith is
saving pennies
in your piggy bank
to buy a present

for someone you love.

Faith is looking for God
and finding His love

in your family and in your friends.

It is looking for God

and finding His love in the nighttime sky,

in the sunrise,

and in the rainbow after a rain.

Faith can be "just knowing"

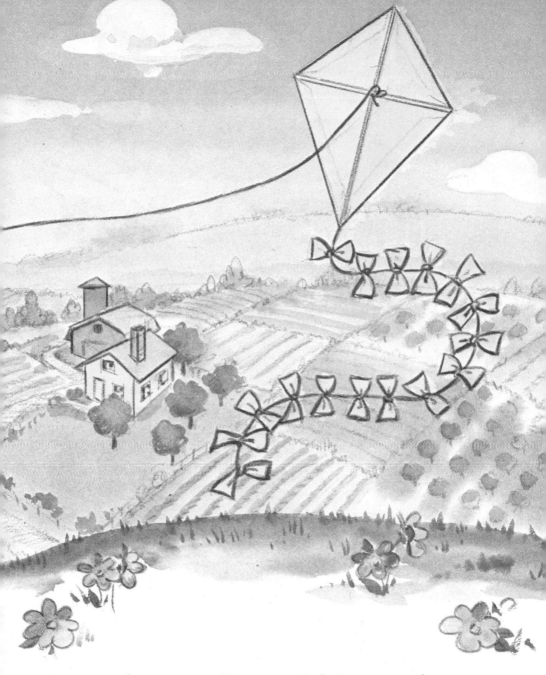

that God's world is good.

"Just knowing" that a bird's song
will be nice to hear.

"Just knowing"
that a kitten
will feel soft and warm.

"Just knowing" that a flower
will have a sweet smell.

Faith is trusting.
Faith is hoping.
Faith is believing.

Faith is depending on God
to keep all of His promises
and saying "Thank You"
because He always does.